APPARENTLY

Matthew Caley's *Thirst* (Slow Dancer, 1999) was shortlisted for the Forward Prize for Best First Collection. Since then he has been Poet-in-Residence at the Poetry Society Café and commended, 3rd and 2nd, in separate National Poetry Competitions. His second full-length collection, *The Scene of My Former Triumph* (Wrecking Ball Press, 2005), was followed by a third, *Apparently* (2010), from Bloodaxe Books. He has also co-edited *Pop Fiction: The Song in Cinema* with Stephen Lannin (Intellect, 2005). In a previous life – in Newcastle – he designed record sleeves including Prefab Sprout's debut, *Swoon*. He now lives, works and writes in London.

MATTHEW CALEY

APPARENTLY

BLOODAXE BOOKS

ISBN: 978 1 85224 863 5

First published 2010 by
Bloodaxe Books Ltd,
Highgreen,
Tarset,
Northumberland NE48 1RP.

www.bloodaxebooks.com
For further information about Bloodaxe titles
please visit our website or write to
the above address for a catalogue.

Supported by
**ARTS COUNCIL
ENGLAND**

Cover design: Neil Astley & Pamela Robertson-Pearce.

Printed in Great Britain by
Bell & Bain Limited, Glasgow, Scotland.

for Pavla, Iris and Mina

'I'm your huckleberry'

> DOC HOLLIDAY [played by Val Kilmer]
> *Tombstone* [Dir: George P Cosmatos, 1993]

'the melodramatic revulsion which characterises this age as insane, the melodramatic enthusiasm which calls it great, are both justified by the swollen incomprehensibility and illogicality of the events which apparently make up its reality. Apparently.'

> HERMANN BROCH
> *The Sleepwalkers*

Q: 'What did the dog's footprint
   say to the horse's footprint?
A: 'Where have our bodies gone?

> DR SIRI ZAMORUVA

'the mechanics of amorous vassalage require a fathomless futility'

> ROLAND BARTHES
> *A Lover's Discourse: Fragments*

ACKNOWLEDGEMENTS

Acknowledgements are due to the following periodicals, publications and websites where some of these poems, or versions of them, previously appeared: *The Independent, The Independent on Sunday, Magma*, www.nthposition.com, *The North*, www.thepoem.co.uk/limelight, *Poetry Review*, www.poetrylondon.co.uk, www.poetrysociety.org.uk and *The Wolf*.

Some of these poems appear in the anthology *Identity Parade: New British and Irish Poets*, edited by Roddy Lumsden (Bloodaxe Books, 2010).

'Nag' was Commended in the Poetry London Competition, 2009; 'L.Z' won 2nd Prize in the National Poetry Competition, 2004; 'The Bluff' was Commended in the *Poetry London* Competition, 2006.

'Nudie the Tailors', 'Late-Nite Taxi-Cab [1517-]', 'The Ambassadors' and 'Louis Quatorze Chairs' were part of an exhibition during a residency at the Poetry Society Café. 'The Duke' was originally written for a photographic project by Kitty O'Shea.

'Illinois Ode' was originally written for Broadcast's '50 States' readings. 'Elbow' was originally commissioned for a silent cinema project by Darlington Arts Centre.

With many thanks to Mr Roddy Lumsden, Mr John Stammers, Mr John Hartley Williams, Mr Matthew Hollis and Mr David Briggs for plangent commentary and much else besides.

CONTENTS

My Prodigious Appetites

Apparently, two centuries to reach this arid plateau,
so long distracted by prodigious appetites
– the thin ones like Modiglianis, the one plump as a Watteau –
I discard their various garments like serviettes.

Thin air. A spit-flecked goat chewing scrim. The city below a rash of lights.
I sit and eat a thick wedge of Black Forest Gâteau.

Threshold

Apparently, after a glass of "hooch"
broached my throat
like a hand-held torch
I felt like stepping forth
into whatever the drip-dry rain bestowed.

I left The Planet
and turned into Elswick Road.

Apparently, after a dram of the Devil's brew
had scorched its fiery trail
like a shaving-rash
across my Adam's apple
I failed entirely to decide

whether to leave The World's End
or step into Milton Rd.

Apparently, seven sips of Hangman's Noose
later, a wave rose in my gorge
like some primordial urge
to yell 'The drink's got me like whomsoevers houri'
all my syllables skewed.

I left The Dragon
and turned into Mulberry Road.

Apparently, after a gulp of ice-bright slivovice
burnt my mouth like a lover's kiss
particles of ash and lint
stung my breath,
so I felt renewed

enough to leave The Globe
and turn into Plato Road.

Apparently, after a glass of absinthe
lifted my head from my neck
like some greeny air-balloon
piloted by Nadar, I saw the world below as like
a glass of absinthe seen from the highest cloud.

I left The Milk Maid
and turned into Salop Street.

Apparently, after a glass of water
so clear I could see my future
in it was fouled by two disintegrating *aspirin*
all began to jitter
as if before the coming of the flood.

I left The Planet
and turned into Elswick Rd

And Therein Lies the Gift

I *Jimmy The Greek*

Apparently, legend has it the Greeks were wont to woo trees –
having done, completely done, with fickle woman,
they took up with some spruce or birch,
stripping the bark from slender, off-white shoulders.
Trees, see, stood their ground;
weren't loose or left you in the lurch,

you could nestle in the fork, encircle the slim waist,
as a sapling welcomes sun-spangles into her arms.
They coveted nothing racier
than acacia or weeping willow
bending to water. Only dryads got them hard.
See, one minute I'm palming him a shrink-wrapped eighth of dope

by Café Pushkar or the Recreation Centre,
next thing, see, he's eloped with this silver birch.

II *Revisiting the Worm*

Apparently, I'd downed the very last gulp of mescal,
swallowing whole the pitiable comma
of worm, then entered a golden realm
– part-Mexican Day of the Dead, part coma –
wherein the worm began to dream
me as an inebriated consul

going down on some dark consuelo of the cabbala,
her iron-ribbed stomach-muscles, the trail of coal-dark down
that led from her navel in a fine, inviting trickle
to collect in a little tombola, where a black swan
with six signets following led me below the water,
below, even, the earth below the water,

beyond the stretch of any dilapidated pier in Dollarton or Brixton.
I tried to articulate my speech-bubbles. What came out was soil.

Apparently, Percy Bysshe Shelley
lost all his children eventually,
sacrificed to wanderlust or craft.
He left barely visible mounds all the way across Europe
like cairns, but marking troughs, not peaks.
Wherever he travelled followed faults and rifts.

From here, he could see the hazy, flattened land mass
of the Meridian beyond – through her eyes, opal-almond
as they were, almond-opal.
Shelley copped it for lack
of an available life-raft, lack of a far-flung guide-rope,
then drowned in sand like Ozymandias.

He knew that gifts
were afflictions. Afflictions, gifts.

Con

Apparently, a late-lit evening, *Zinfandel*, windows open on South
London, two Size-Zero hoes in slub-silk robes, both
lookers – one a gamin, one a fly-girl – reflecting on a gloss in *Elle*.
Outside, automatons at raves hear
bass-notes shimmer in their ears.

Dear houris, neo Know-it-alls,
loll all you like in Yates's
Wine Lodge – *the innocent and the beautiful*
have no enemy but time. Thom Yorke said that. Or else Tom Waits.

Both beautiful – one a *Gitane*, one a garnet.

Not one of you has conviction but all of you feel guilt.
Someone's ghost written everything you've felt.
You can't even spell 'gazebo'
let alone build one. Mine's a *Bud*, some *Lucky Strikes*, an itch, an eighth
       of blow.

The Butterfly

Apparently inconsolable, Maude Gonne gone,
finding power and abuse of power in the bent neck of a swan,
he sits at the tower's window-ledge
having half-eaten only of the Salmon of Knowledge,
its spine exposed to a toothcomb: hence, sheep-cells, monkey-glands,
            whatever might restore
the sense of her, become the prick, the spur
to bring on visions: himself Plain Bill
perhaps, sharing a tower block squat in Brixton, 1991, bending to the spill,

taking his turn at the toke. The flame doubles, trebles in the silver-foil
ad infinitum. Later, he nuzzles
the ear of some green-eyed gazelle,

some skimpy Pallas Athene and somehow swallows her butterfly. It drops
            the length of his duodenum
echoey as a burnished gong. Its taste, bitter, recalls a verdigris Astrodome
in Byzantium. And Maude Gonne gone.

Late-Nite Taxi Cab [1517–   ]

Apparently, you say 'Follow that cab!', or is it, perhaps, a hearse
sliding on heat-haze mirage or oil slick of black ice
while the neon-lit names float by as though
a finger is stroking an index,
allowing nothing to linger
– Chaucer Close, Marvell Close, Shakespeare Close, Earl of Wessex –
what a parade of knee-garters caught in our rear-view mirror.
'Follow that cab!' is the cry, as if you're Alphonse de Lamartine
with all his epic propensity to fail.

Yet the river sweats no oil,
merely sifts its weeds of spidery neon
to squeegee time and history from our
crazy windscreen, snake and go. Neither is there a wail of high tenor-sax
as me and *les girls*, breast-plated and plaited as ladette-Boadiceas, feel
        somehow we're under the aegis of some harbinger
– follow that cab! – some harbinger or hex,
or else on the brink of a monumental breakthrough
as when, irked by the quantitative gait of his horse,
the Earl of Surrey sat down to invent blank verse.

Difficult Third Album

I *For Howard Devoto*

Apparently, the sound of a glacial stream or the great flows.
The trace a glacier leaves behind like a flaw.
No face since Isidore Ducasse
has calcified to such a carapace
or summoned what the curled-up fossil knows;
that is, everything time has been through. We can't suppose,
what with the world turning, that a stalagmite under the Northern Pole
isn't a stalactite under the Southern. So, no matter how we extol

the arctic tern, when a glacier moves, grit in its wake,
no one hears. No one hears the popping of bladderwrack
in the pebbled gulley. No one hears a glacier toil.

Not the passing fleet with their silos of whale-oil
run low. Not that scuppered hull. What time has lost
we summon as we skirt the permafrost.

II *The Pointer Sisters*

Apparently, smoky triumvirate, the three,
lip-synching to snub-nosed microphones, literally breathing *Fire*,
hip-bones rolling in perpetuity
in denial of this denial of desire,
alluding to the Old Testament, alluding to Shakespeare,
in Afro-wigs or with real Afro hair, separate yet so in unity
I can hear that radio, see that car,
smell the warm seat-leather, see

it peel layer after layer. O Three Graces of the disco-age, may no mirror
ball disperse your easy glamour. Our one entreaty
is – do not reform, do not disturb the for-

maldehyde of YouTube. Then safely can we say 'They breathed fire,
were themselves like three flames wavering.' How easy
it is to show that we don't care.

III *The Smell of Leonard Cohen*

Apparently is redolent of *kohl*-eyed demimondaines
opening up the blind
at 5.00 A.M.
precisely. The cigar-smoke of some borscht-veldt comedian
backstage, stepping
out of puddled lame;
or maybe ethanol, the ferment of slightly-bruised flesh.
You can catch it off any easterly when most alone,

smuggle it into your mind like a fickle wish.
Or else a turd inching
its way through the whole nine yards of colon

which, after the requisite pause,
scientists will lay out in a Petri-dish
in order to pick out diamonds.

IV *The Duke*

Apparently, the sutures healed perfectly post-op.
A Swiss clinic. Vast sheets of glass. Rivulets of rain.
The view through it an empty street in Brixton.
The latest white label beneath your arm. The Rosetta Stone.

You had it all: the hair, the bones.
Helga's bee-stung pout and a Lucky Strike. Your full six stone.
The tick-tock pulse of a Trans-European train.
Crowley's goat. Nazi-plunder. *Golden Years. Wop, wop, wop.*

V *Closer*

Apparently Ian Curtis, haunted, much-vaunted singer with Joy Division
was watching whichever Herzog
happens to feature a suicide
on video
the very night – split between girlfriend and wife – the very night
he took his own life.

Purely in the spirit of 'What if?', what if
he'd been watching *Fitzcarraldo* instead, he might not now be dead,
dead these twenty-odd years, embalmed in the slate-
grey packaging of *Still*,
in hock to neo-Gothic angst, epilepsy, drugs,
but pushing some vast steamboat up a dew-stippled, rain-

filled river, in the South Americas somewhere – a mote,
a parakeet, a climbing tendril.

Towpath Ode

Apparently, had I not, *my innamorata*, outlined my suit
so suitably, from the dump-truck's mound of soil
to the towpath where the elderberry ignited,
your iPod might not have ignited with *Soul II Soul*?
We were alone, abroad in the world
by the lank canal that served as the spine of a city

where men sat in waterproof suits
caught little of significance. That bridge matched half-circle
to half-circle, making a full, deigning
to mimic either moon or sun. We made a pledge of solidarity
then drew each other into each other's world,
falling between the wolfberry and a building site

in an utter froth. Afterwards you set out
to climb the inner circle of the bridge, bare-handed, me at loss
to describe the in-curve of your body's design
against the stone – cornerstone? – lodestone? – hanging in solid air
upended whilst the cherry-blossom swirled
hectically. That instant we both gained second-sight.

The proof reader of this ode follows suit,
missing a vital comma, the comma between 'possibility' and 'blood-cell'
in the original draft, after either *fata morgana* or *ignis
fatuus*, where it wriggles – part-tadpole, part lodestar –
into a semi-circle to form a spine. We wake, for all the world
like any other sightseers

having left the safe path for the wild path, having split
the atom of each other and fused. Nearby some druid with sickle
is slashing the hackberry ignominiously
as my iPod ignites the tinnitus of *De La Soul*,
whilst you, *my innamorata*, having been offered the world,
make do with only a city, this wild, this wortleberry spray.

Cover Up

Apparently, though you'd not notice,
the way snow and ice
are enticed

onto a silver birch branch,
so the top-half is white,
the lower half darker,

is pure replication, the replication
of nature. For any silver birch branch
worth its salt

is already white on its upper half,
dark below, the inverse of this night,
hugely dark, above this sheet, this pillow.

How oft in annotated legend
does some deracinated Greek or other
dump his spouse – just like that –

to shack-up with some slender birch
or witch-hazel,
forsaking all human attention.

                *

Here is the ice-shagged birch tree
beyond a lawn stiff and spry as *Astroturf*,
here its one, off-season bed

topped with white silt,
underlain with grit. Here's me
fingering the flayed spine

of Louis Zukofsky,
pondering how each
drench or douse

becomes a stalagmite
equally poised, yet petrified,
not that you'd notice.

Tojo the Dwarf

Apparently, the day will come when we cross that bridge
emblazoned with TOJO THE DWARF –
its mobile of midges,
tyre-swing, dank canal beneath; its nettled edges,
rusted sidings, fishermen catching condoms, industrial froth;

that bare wolfberry bush on the worn-out towpath –
all seem to side with him, dew-wet though the sedge is.
Much will they make of it, these purveyors
of urban-myth, when we cross that bridge
emblazoned with TOJO THE DWARF.

England, My England

...the brick April might throw at the school-run
is not yet airborne when
rumours
of a puma
loose in Carshalton Beeches
reach us. *Apparently*.

The Mule for Real

(i.m. K.S.)

Apparently, the mule
shot-off like a half-cocked blunderbuss
at the cry of 'woooaahhh!' from the tentative muleteer,
left for dead in a scrub of gorse or columbine. Ever was it thus:
the law as is and the mule
as mutineer, chewing the forbidden thistle.
They want his ribs for marrow, his nuts, his sinews for gristle;
they want his belly-
tripe, his jawbone for broth

to boil in a pot to a spurious froth
whey-thin and utterly bilious;
to grind those bones with a mortar and pestle
to render a chalk-white talcum. Yet will he essay epistle after epistle,
anti-tract and anti-dictate, fly-whisk tail
rotating in its stall. So, whether disguised as poet, prophet, badass,
seer, ever was it thus: the tenderfoot muleteer
left holding his fraying lily-rope, left in a scrub of hollyhocks or furze,
and a rip in the sky the exact same size as a mule.

Circular Error Probability

Apparently, policy-wonks 'do lunch'.
Tim Buckley yells 'Hallelujah!'
Bush Senior's out on his ranch.
There's phosphorus in Fallujah.

Jeff Buckley sings 'Hallelujah'.
Wheels part from their axles.
There's phosphorus in Fallujah.
A child's head turns to pixels.

Wheels part from their axles.
An autocue scans its reader.
A child's head turns to pixels.
Technocrats quote Derrida.

An autocue blanks its reader.
Some hoodie reads *Guns 'n' Ammo*.
A plutocrat scorns Derrida.
Slipknot play *Guantanamera*.

Some hoodies quote *Odi Et Amo*.
John Snow has lost his earpiece.
Slipknot play at Guantanamo
Bay. A sales-run on army surplus.

There's a sales-run on army surplus.
A hilltop of shins and ankles.
John Snow has lost his equipoise.
Mohammad has lost six uncles.

Mohammad has lost six uncles.
A fifth of Bourbon and branch.
A hilltop of shins and ankles.
Journalists reel from the stench.

The Trident deal is a cinch.
A still wind ruffles the night-jar.
Bush Junior's out on his ranch.
There's phosphorus in Fallujah.

By the Water-cooler

Apparently, we gather by the water-cooler
as the city, through blinds, vibrates with drills, ignor-
ing the ploughed-water sound of police launches on the river.
'Yes', we say, to some fellow water-cooler loiterer
– What weather! What peristalsis! – as if the water in the water-cooler
had distilled itself from the speckled condensation on the wing-mirrors
of ambulances. In the calm before
the fire alarm we seek solace in a tank of nothingness, in the temp sent to water
the plastic fern, from the domino-fall of box-files, computer error,
to dizziness at the vastness of America.
When the news breaks, percipient with sirens, we aver,
pale Romans at the spa
to gather by the water-cooler.

Surveillance

I *The Stipend*

Apparently, those last exiled breaths as long as her spine
were formed by the gaze of a beaten man,
sarcophagi for the mind,
a golden statuette where nothing is won.
Niet. Nothing. For someone or something has filled in
her bikini of un-sunburn,
my loose comma of hair, my 'ladies' gun',
this unhinged world dependent on a pun.
I long for every pixel of her skin,
and burrow through to mine
a deeper theme –
a pile of soil in Hoagy Carmichael's skull, my stipend,
woman as Tutankhamun,
a solid bar of light in a hotel room.

II *Safe House*

Apparently, the dust-motes on the dust-covers are straight out of Le Carré –
the gun gaffer-taped under the lavatory lid
which isn't obviously there, a Luger or Beretta
– that aforementioned "ladies' gun" –
but no trace at all of sloe-eyed Titania, her of the velveteen choker,
the key, the knee-stocking, the pout, the real politik.
You dial and the world's answer phones are on,
unspooling their messages: *Merry Christmas and a Happy New Year,*
We're not in right now. Mother about the drains, as always;
your sisters draining stock. You'd kill for anyone who pays,
for envelopes in unmarked notes, an aura for hire.
Here, the air that hovers around and under the chairs is full of aeons
and lint, the chairs themselves stacked
tensely display that certain density we look for
but rarely get in our murky world where "losses" equal "gains",
where the dead letter office offers us no dead letter
from the forces you continue to elude.
This poem is being texted to you from the boot of a stolen car.

To Thee, Quintilius

Apparently, Quintilius, inept consul not finding anyone faithful to betray,
take to your pergola, the In-tray out-towering the Out-tray.

*

To thee, Quintilius, the gloss is off the grapes of the sweet Republic –
take to your colonnaded rooms, all your apes otiose and sick.

*

Apparently, Quintilius, iPod crammed with songs of epic yearning
shuffled, quit that bath-house karaoke, quit that vapid gurning.

*

To thee, Quintilius, consul of the inconsolable, grief is vent
only when such grief can be perceived as an "event".

*

Apparently, Quintilius, slave-power powers your quinquereme – no need
of bilious sails.
Your vine stocks wither. Your pantry is polluted by snails.

*

To thee, Quintilius, your Rubicon is ruined and your runnel –
bedecked mare mounted by a stallion. Your eyes ride postillion.

*

Apparently, Quintilius, much foams beneath your white, censorious toga,
though nothing will suffice. Go sacrifice a goat.

Louis Quatorze Chairs

Apparently, *my innamorata*, much happens around Louis Quatorze chairs:
drip-dry semen exchanges, bevels, photo opportunities, court intrigues,
that saffron-yellow monkey; the odd, delicate beheading;
everything within its aura or orbit
– all actual matter, *my innamorata*, all data
transmogrified into an epoch
– making exclamation such as 'My concubine,
the morphology of your bustle exacerbates my libido
by degrees',

or some such folly. Thus, amongst the expansiveness of empirical cushions
       we are as fleas,
by the puffed-up lilos that float the municipal lido
and its crazy-paving sheen
where monumental orrery adhere to our seats like cushions stuffed with capoc.
So caught between star-fucker or stellar-mater
we dally and wait,
my innamorata, to contemplate soft furnishing and inexpensive bedding
into which everything sinks and segues,
not least the munitions factory, tin-tacks, and, of course, occasionally,
       Louis Quatorze.

Onyx Bedposts

Apparently, I have loitered here deadbeat,
tensed for her tread,
a thrashing crocodile in the Orient Wheat
trying to trade the aberrant thought for the deed,
knowing she will show me as much mercy
as Monsieur Swann was shown
by Odette de Crécy,
there, upon her odorous divan before her cover was blown –
Supposedly, my masterpiece was completed with a yawn
during prolonged abstinence from sex,
or with the arborescence seen
at the heart of an onyx,
as anyone
for whom you'd plight your troth
turns out to be an invert, a courtesan
or both...
I am author of the eternal whim.
My sentences will furnish you a room
full of vetiver and slap
where even "en hiver" the nymphs go commando or bright green,
hold a candelabrum up to aimlessness...my one, true aim.
The Ducal line has ended in a milksop.
– a cover as thin as that bodice of whale-bone or crêpe-de-chine
she swaps for another such
behind a Chinese screen,
opaque as her it hides. One touch
another three months later, the hindsight of regret, then
birdsong, a botched duel, the cool embrace of the Seine.

The Ambassadors

Apparently, they're come to peer pensively at some improvised Lady Godiva,
are taking swigs from indiscreet hip-flasks, half-full,
half-empty of Schnapps. They know the giving that famishes the taker,
        the undertaking that famishes the giv-
er. We find them in their element and their cups, yet still able
to argue whether to have the Ouija-board
outlawed,
whether the noonday
sun is flashing
off a spun coin,

or a spun coin
is flashing
off the sun, the any-
angled storefronts flimsy as balsawood backdrops. And yet because their
        running-boards
are garlanded with horseshit, their purring limousine seems untoward,
has all the makings of a hearse. Ermine-muffs cruise past called Hortense
        or Mabel,
yell 'Hello, love' – as if they've ever met it – 'Hello, love'.
Suddenly, they want to slip, slip into something more comfortable –
negligees, perhaps, or the river.

The Prediction

Apparently, I will die at twenty-nine,
much like Christopher Marlowe in his tavern-brawl.
My despair will be as real
as that of Alphonse de Lamartine
when dumped by Madame Charles
at the enervating spa of Aix-les-Bains.
On the mountain's slope, in an old oak's shade,
in mood melancholic I sit me down.

On such dark matter do I brood –
softened so by certainty, often though erroneous
and injurious to others. The pages of my book have come undone.

    *

You find me eleven years beyond my own prediction
bathing one evening in my own bright blood –
the failsafe method practised by Plotonus.

Between Commissions for Russian Aristocrats

Apparently, the path is wayward with sedge and spiky whitethorn,
and you suffer the length of it as one might suffer an ache,
the novel in your knapsack
– in lieu of nourishment – being the heavier burden.
You are sporting boots with sable-trim, muddy
and sodden, as if sable boot-trim disqualifies you from history, gout,
having to work machinery, the languorous onset
of the Pox. Revolution makes you giddy,

but enough of the playground swings. Being headless gives you credibility.
The salons are full of whores, muffs, odours
and Olga with that cachou on her tongue. When you enter the immaculate city

the book escapes your knapsack like a bird, goes airborne
over roofs. Later, you sleep in a vale of cedars
or the crook of an ox-bow lake. *Wait for it, wait for it.*

Between Women

Apparently, as a sapling
    might sway in relation
to another bow-bent sapling
    in a stiffening wind, so is this similar
to what can appertain
        between women.

There are eyes, below those, these days, the midriff
    giving out a level stare
as like or not to another midriff
    – pierced or otherwise – one on one:
fixed points of an invisible umbilical
        between women.

Though men get hard, hard as teak or oak,
    still their lack
grows to an exquisite pain,
    yet never quite as hard by comparison
as certain glances
        exchanged between women

behind their backs. Foul man follows foul man,
    enough never being enough,
crawling through life like a terrapin,
    bawling in the buff;
the low beasts they become
        between women.

A ceiling-fan begins a quiet revolution,
    bears witness
to the downward rustle of dropped dress
    and dropped dress; legs stand, plush or apart;
air makes its movement
        beneath and between women.

Apparently, the wide and witless mezzanine
        of heaven is not canopy enough
to cover or contain us – glimpse and untruth only – yet halcyon
        and hush govern in equal measure
whenever I have lain
            between women.

Maidenhair Fern

Apparently, this hot house holds a maidenhair fern
so beautiful that sane men kneel before it,
its spry aerated vigour and spiral arch
getting them parched in the mouth, flush under the collar
the air around it speckled with pheromones.
The fern itself was born of a special splice
between two competing strains
nitrogen–fixed and swatched,
lain upon a bed of the softest compost

a rare specimen of which any knowing botanist would boast.
Here, at Eden, we keep it under 24-hour watch,
stern guards on rotation, and no one
gets to see it. Until the night, one man and his accomplice
abseil down through the hothouse Astrodome,
gently manhandle the fern, disappear
into spore–riddled air. *Sweet fern, as you rub yourself against the bark-flayed birch,*
as we brace against each other in the dirt,
the dew is on us and won't now be shaken.

Pines Again

Apparently, you sang *'Where Did You Sleep Last Night? I Lay Under the Pines'*
by Leadbelly, he of the tar-pit, gut-bucket blues
with the lightest skip, of the prison-pail,
of white-noise field recordings sang it as we lay
under actual pines and saw, almost piningly,
them seem as giant aerials
seeking a jag of lightning
from somewhere "so out there" in the blank sheet of the sky
like *The Lightning Field* by Walter De Maria,

knowing that however high we reach we could never reach any higher
than ourselves, than the yelped cry of a Leadbelly,
than the pure future frightening
the present. The sky was aerosol-
blue the day we at last got married under *The Lightning Field*, yet a spray
of rain or vapour-trails still made us delay,
as a judge might delay the decision to let a Leadbelly out on bail.
Where did you sleep last night? Our heads lay on a copy of *Living the Blues*,
our little feet propped on a copse of pines.

Portrait d'une Femme with Sombrero Breast-shield

Apparently, notwithstanding *alpha-fetoprotein*,
your black V-neck jumper is pulled out at
an angle, the breast exposed,
its mauve-purple aureole, another mouth already there,
as beautiful as yours, greedier even than mine. It hurts.
I see the wild magnolia outside, fleshy-pink;
piercing sunrays pixel the pavement below.
A Dalmatian happens under. The dots first align, then misalign.
The dog has disappeared.

I lurch on the periphery. I've read my Freud.
Somewhere in the story I eat my malign
rival. Your nipple has enlarged to a dark sloe.
In the sink,
like lily-pads adrift, *Sombrero* breast-shields float
accusingly. O you Dark Lady beyond compare,
Sister Mercynth and Sister Sandra deliver us! My left nipple is also bruised,
but by my own heart from the inside out.
I haven't a leg to stand on.

Bedrock

Apparently, bedrock lines the alluvial
valley here, ditchwort and stitchwort teem
and through them occasionally flit mayflies or flame-throated birds.
Any geologist collecting specimens might
covet the feldspar and fluorspar
strewn about this terrain,
might cup a glowworm palm to their spark and fire.
But what the prospector
pans out –

the quick-flit, throat-flash of nearly jewellery – might turn out
not to stay. Too brash. Too bright. Yet notice how the river here
deftly shoulders its lights, easing them artfully over rock fall or weir
to where a certain someone steps in
their given once. Fluorspar and feldspar: these two seem to want to linger
longer here. So, when at low-light
naked they come to my chamber – smooth-bellied, taut-ribbed –
never has bedrock seemed
more mercurial or beautiful.

Elbow

Apparently, Clara Bow,
if your face were any nearer, by the neon-green light of the EXIT-
sign we could possibly make out, make out
your famous mouth, big as a house
in which is sat
the entire audience, vibrat-
ing like the F-holes of a cello to know
the exact timbre, the tremolo of your voice. Even your intestinal gurgles emit
from an orchestra pit. For we now know

that 'bosom' shares a root with 'obedient', as in 'to bow'.
Clara, as the light
is somewhat clearer now
we can glimpse you on the Ferris wheel at Lunar Park, a star in orbit,
your feather-boa the after-trail of a comet;
know that space
is the only place where true silence exists. So long. So long may you pirouette
and shimmer there in solace. Sweet, dumb Clara Bow, your kiss was just a
        Foley-artist
chewing their own elbow.

Sojourn in Mantua

Apparently, the raindrops here, spattering the acanthus,
are as big as ping-pong balls
as we tether our runnelled nags to the birch gazebo.
Equine necks give graze to the counterpane.
Thus, we broach the manse, an echoic mile-long atrium,
sole occupant a bay tree, green head swollen with thought;
boldly try the latch of the Master's bedroom.
The next few seconds elongate into aeons.

A four-poster, scorch-red coverlet, flame-lit. You knelt upright,
some man behind, biting your neck, forefinger in your anus
up to the knuckle. Two frock-coated equerries each side giving level gaze.

Your expression mixes shyness, shame and a growing, unwilled
fervour. It obliterates six centuries of calumny and battle.
We know now that nothing will ever save us.

Upside Down

Apparently Ezra Pound would lay at languorous angles on the inevitable
    chaise-longue
– feet up, head down – believing as he did
that so prone his seminal fluid would flow from his testicles to his forehead,
    thus energising
the brain. He gave new meaning to "getting laid".
Hard to tell, in this topsy-turvy paradigm,
which is pubic-hair, what whisker,
the after-trace of the abject, the after-trace of the sublime –
i.e. his *Hieratic Head* by Gaudier-Brzeska.

Older, we find more things to arouse us
not less. Pound spent his last ten years in silence,
all his thinking deep inside his trousers.

Your ghost stalks the living room, barely wearing a silk sarong,
a swoosh of tinnitus.
Touch my forehead, its cranial swell, I've been upside down for too long.

Chinatown Dessert Spoon

'Apparently, only English rain could slant like this,' said Miss Li Po –
like grained rice: half-sleet, half-hail,
or the bamboo-curtain we part to broach this place – of all venues –
scouring the courses for half a quail

stuffed with apricots. Later, your already oval face
beneath its square-cut fringe ballooned like liquid mercury in the dessert-
       spoon. 'The bill,'
you said, half-heartedly, still surveying the menu
with as much steely will

as Ezra Pound might once have surveyed a Fenollosa ms.
for that line about the *'twirling moustaches'*, that line about the *'swallow's tail'*.

Dildo

(after Ezra Pound)

Apparently, onyx, burnished
by Ottoman craftsmen, about a yard long;
you too she has lain aside for an unfinished
game of Mah Jong.

L.Z.

Apparently, born of a hinny and her ass
he hee-haws awesomely; of the little words and letters
like 'A' and 'and' and 'as', and yet, – alas, alack –
never saw the major work complete; of sawhorses
strung with lanterns in a Brooklyn
Street – where two 'As made the 'M' of the Latin word 'manes'
and therein made their manes; inverted they made 'W' for 'Will', the Bard –
[he pondered, exclusively on his Bottom], of the city that never sleeps,
of whom another dared to think a geodesic dome, à la mode

over New York like an atmosphere solidified –
that never sleeps except for the zed-zed-zeds of the fire-escapes;
of barely scraping his room and board
to light the low gas-flame or 'the live flame
of tradition', wherein they brook no line
that doesn't sing as such: 'If seahorses
could but sing Offenbach, Father' – alas, alack –
of a man who for forty-six years watered a single letter,
was left with nothing but the odour of odourless zinnias.

Nag

Apparently, no horse is here,
no horse heir-apparent to this air. No horse of gut and withers, hind-legs
haltered to an ash, no eyes chrome-brown
with longing so unfathomable to man,
nay, no horse is here. No horse is hereby
evident by the hedgerow or the hawthorn tree
shifting the world entirely with each shift of ham or hock.
Maybe given to Bedlam, tethered to bedrock, gone to glue
or gristle, whatever, here-

in stands no horse. Any Admiral or Emperor
cemented in the Square, whose head bears not a tricorn but a traffic-cone,
        would bid adieu
to any such burdensome beast, any such scrofulous crock
with farcy on his leg, scree
inside his hoof, a coat of mange and flea,
left to blink under blinkered lanterns
that slowly illuminate Night Town,
wherein the diggers have dug, the laundress left. STREET CLOSED. Go beg
a bridle path, a towpath or an arching orchard. No horse is here.

Cy Twombly

Apparently, where drawing and writing combine, therein lay the theme –
a notebook of scribbles, a chalk-line
down a wall fusing together
as sea and sky become indecipherable.
Thereby, on the late-night overland in Camden, England or Camden USA,
the taggers' lasso gets spritz-sprayed
by orange-overall'd workmen into something approaching abstraction.
These be the words of poets and philosophers –
where a line squitters, betrays itself, flits, erases

any distinction between saw-tooth conifer
and cyan-azure, bulldozer
and Snowcem'd wall, they seem to say: to not act in isolation
from each other, to even out debts owed or never paid
might one day even become us –
the miles of overhead cable
that run in parallel-lines to the point at which they gather
in the angled nib of a pen,
therein might we cite and say 'Cy Twombly'.

Queneau Repository

Apparently, from the arcane windows of the Queneau Repository
we hear a pea-hen longing for her proud peacock
in his ring-fenced, Louis Quatorze ruff and spurs.
Ours is the transitory fate
– gables, common-agricultural implements, corn-stalks –
which makes us side somewhere with the pea-hen's longing,
a piercing cry as sad as the saddest song
by the saddest chanteuse – with her one colonic suppository,
her one Manalo Blah-Blah-Blah-nik,
all ignoble longing is hers; with her gilded walk,
her hat of raffish taffeta
she is bound to utter 'rats are rhizomes' quoting 'Jacques Deleuze'.
Some wild, implacable Duchess hunting for a tinted contact lens on her knees,
utterly deshabille but for bling,
is having a tête à tête
with the shoes of some Senior Euro-Tory,
slightly soiled as they are with peacock-cack
which she sniffs with the hauteur of one sniffing crack-
cocaine. He is here for 'talks about talks about talks'
– here being this fake-marble reception, wisteria-sprigs outré as hell in their
        neo-Classical urns –
with the French Ambassador and the Irish Taoiseach
in what, he demurs, will be 'a very long innings'.
He has stashed some bonds in a numbered safety-deposit
box – 5-3-2-6-1-4 – then glimpsed his fate
in the complicated twists and turns of a Pecan & Maple plait,
his morning coffee's milk-
swirl, as he takes 'the long view' from a moulting balcony.
The svelte concierge who has his ear
and will not give it back murmurs 'langue and parole', 'parole and langue',
telling him of the sly peruque and oil-oval eyes of one Georges Perec,
his surplus-mountain of Es. Some patroness taking a pack-
wagon to the pergola, mapping out her inevitable route
with a series of 'seminal cairns' à la Richard Long,
careers through the corn-stalks
as if on the Grand Tour;

for, no matter how many theoretical questions we posit,
we still skirt the hem of the Queneau Repository,
finding buttons in tram-cars, buttons in bulk
pecked by a ruff-bedecked peacock into the unfamiliar.

Norwegian Jarlsberg

Apparently, contains no artificial flavourings
as it waits here – blister-packed, shrink-wrapped –
in all its slightly-dented, mild-yellow nothing-
ness. Opened, drawn, then quartered, it will first impede
your thoughts, then mould them. What curds have been through to come
      to this.
It's 2.00 A.M. A low-wattage hum from the purblind fridge.
Chequered-tiles. The one that lunar light likes to polish.
This cheese-knife, its keen, serrated edge.

You will wake, sweating through muslin, talking Norwegian
to anyone who'll listen – Norwegians, mostly –
on a trawler-filled dockside, feeling waxy and wooden

as prime *Norwegian Jarlsberg*. There's something about the quarter-moon
hung above you – whey-faced, listless, ghostly –
that looks like a slither of rind. They find you asleep in the kitchen.

Objects

Apparently, objects act as alibi to the immediate,
a seamless invisibility we're
emptied by. Enter Mr Ken Osis, branch manager,
doyen of tree-like thought, tie the colour of chlorophyll
surrounded by Japanese pudenda as if in a diorama.
'Pudenda,' he says, 'are not on my immediate agenda',
circumscribed as he is by MOR-balladry,
its ritornellos pure sign,
the latest Diva in head-set surrounded by baffles

singing so stridently the whole studio might collapse inward as a soufflé.
Thus, the surrounding real is vacuumed up by the luminous screen
at its centre, dispersed through ether-cables by a vast machinery
transparent as glar
by whichever psychopomp of whatever psychodrama
we have need to re-fill
with certain stock archetypes as reified by Freud. I stand under a tanager
not knowing whether I transmit or if I am a transmitter,
bodiless objects teeming in my interior. *Post it.*

Three Ways to Crash the Car

I

Apparently, giddy Randall Jarrell
one dank, wry night
lit out for the highway,
found his last embrace in the oncoming fender
of an Oldsmobile. Become a floundering avatar
it ended with his forehead imprinted
with the number-plate.

II

Apparently, poor old Frank O'Hara
took a stroll along the glamorous sand
behind the Hamptons,
his liver excoriated, his heart foggy,
exhausted by stray lambs and illegal tender
a single kiss or piece of luck
would easily have felled him. Let alone a beach-buggy.

III

Apparently, feisty, half-recovered Jackson Pollock was
at least behind the wheel
of his own automobile
when he wrapped it around a copse of alders,
in fact, wrapped everything up, with metal like cellophane,
bruise-blues and cochineal. 'I am nature,'
he'd once said. He became nature again.

The Host

Apparently, we are fashionably late to the pre-empted event, the soirée
our tinctures of lime and laudanum or whatever,
well, like a Grade-A coke-encrusted glass-rim,
or is it *Tate & Lyle Snowcem*'d over?
The host imbues us all with such a sense of WELCOME,
like a boot on a WELCOME-mat. Welcome, Matt,
– it's Matthew actually, two Ts please – as
we slump by the trestle-tables of little bites
and vol-au-vents

so weightless they float off their surfaces like pingpong balls over air-vents.
Our name-tags the flesh made word. It's
like the required rooms themselves are releas-
ing for interim decant and fenestration. We might
mooch for aeons around this here enormous Astrodome
fashionably late, in cognate resource clusters
airily disengage as *Jules et Jim*,
whilst our host has the sly glance of a cantilever
prising, one tilt and we all get erased.

What Now?

I *Now*

Apparently 'now' isn't, strictly, often 'now', mainly mostly it's 'then' –
sacred groves rather than zinc counters, at its zenith

no kitsch lava-lamps, cyberspace, zits, zeitgeists, Lara Croft
only the zealous cosseting of craft.

To own *Dolby* octophonic but speak in mono
espressos like black-holes against the table's moon.

Homer's hinterland, passé-pastorals, metastrophes, Roman cast-offs,
the after trace of epic like a wormcast.

Meanwhile, saplings sway inside their sleeves of mesh.
Bark peels back in sappy quarters for dryads with no shame.

All the young men making *'free translations'*.
All the women working on their *'versions'*.

II *What?*

Apparently, Miss En-Abyme said 'O my allergies against the everyday!'
so we felt the abject ecstasy of the inured.
That's when we tried the ouija board.
As the radio told us gently of pile-ups and delay

Miss En-Abyme and I embraced the table. The glass slid instantly,
spelling out a forty-two point Scrabble
score – *Cicatrix* maybe the word was – conjuring up James Merrill
who, clutching a marmoreal bust of Pallas Athene

said 'Subtlety's over-rated, poesie needs to be gay!'
O our allergies against the everyday.

Squibs

I *The Spirit of the Age*

Apparently, the spirit of French chanson is preserved by government
edict as mantra, as myth.
They have exhumed Yves Montand
and are reading his teeth.

II *Favourite Love Poems*

Apparently, the ultimate perversion available to mere mortals,
got up like some gecko in a VR helmet,
enumerates the binary and Apollinaire's nine portals,
slick with skin-sensors in his dildo-suit.

III *Religion*

Apparently, un-pruned
the apple-boughs hung so low that spring
the settlers had to walk face down to the ground
as if in obeisance to everything.

IV *Stalker*

Apparently, by the latest position of the sun
my shadow should be lying in the foreground,
and yet it's nowhere to be seen.
I will take some other shadow from behind.

V *The Book of Exodus*

Apparently, we acquire a route-map of the exodus from Egypt,
delicately hieroglyphed on wafer-thin papyrus,
which leads us, circuitously, out of the ill-lit crypt,
guided by the gas-flame of a single iris.

Dayrush

Apparently the
mind seeks out its slyest thought
in taut syllables.

Hip-hop tinnitus.
Birds on municipal-bins.
Sensemelia.

Sink-estate neon.
Smell of *Dreft*. LAUNDRETTE-sign run-
ny in a puddle.

Planes. Asphalt. White-lines.
The road as if a river
mirrors vapour-trails.

Seven [or five] *Coronas*,
each primed with a raw-fleshed lime,
go off like fireworks.

Such replenishment
as Rihaku might have found
in meandering.

Such meanderings
as Rihaku might have made
to replenish loss.

Morleys chicken-bone
carried by a flighty dog
with only three legs.

Dawn is a goer
not by Twombly. Spray-gun spurt.
The wind is feedback.

Thin saplings in mesh
teeter as a young girl first
inside her stockings.

Beer-bottle opened
in the crack of a door-hinge.
Pop! An arc of froth.

Way Out West

I *Nudie the Tailors*

Apparently, between Laredo High Street
and the lightning, a lone cartwheel
of tumbleweed lit out for parts unknown. We'd heard all about
Gram Parsons – the ice, the fire – imagined
a pyre of Nudie shirts, heard the rhinestones cracking
like chestnuts on a brazier. Nudie the Tailors, specialist purveyors
of jewel-encrusted cowboy wear
as first preened and paraded by The Flying Burrito Brothers.
On that rickety Greyhound you needed a tube of Settlers

over a hilltop track redolent of a rattler.
Your insides went feathery. We were tracking the Founding Fathers
over empty basketball courts replete with burnt-out tyre,
Judas tree and an ash-shattered acre,
led by the tutelary spirit of Ramblin' Jack
Elliott, his like and kind, his ilk, chanting *This Land Is Your Land*
to a huddle of nil and his dog. Then you lit out,
went AWOL or West in a mule-cart
and nothing now will ever salve this hurt. Except, perhaps, a Nudie shirt.

II *Poor Papa Peckinpah*

Apparently, see, Senor García, low-rent Lothario
he deflower El Jeres' daughter
and El Jeres, see, well, he want revenge. Cue Bennie, measuring time in tequila-
sips, hard
as hard, looking in wide fly-shades like a long, black fly
himself... then pages of dust-flies... pages of gunfire...
the screenplay here, see, blotched by a bloody thumbprint
that strangely forms the shape of a Mescal-spring.
See. I blink and subliminally hear a car crashing.

Tho' this bruised cactus carries the first flush of spring,
see the barefoot, barbarous children try to hang
a live chicken from the bent
branch of a Judas tree, unaware
of the low, seismic rumble in the throat of the sky
as it says: *Take it, but take it hard –*
let exit the unrelenting rascal
talking to a head in a picnic basket, bowed by feud and fire-water
and no hope now of the seacoast, the unhinged hammock. Or Katie Jurado.

III *Roadrunner Ode*

Apparently, Wile E. Coyote,
you and me are pledged hereafter to give repetitious chase unto – a chicken!
– *beep-beep!* – to bask in his nebulous slipstream
as if in desire is the need to obtain, but also, inbuilt, the need to refrain
        from obtaining.
Refrain-*beep-beep!* How oft have I trod this road to find it the sky,
to drop into the paprika-coloured canyon,
to raise that soft chrysanthemum of dust. How oft do I spark that gelignite
to find it set beneath me. How oft am I blown-up
into pixels of lint and light. For Fate will always whack me –

an anvil delivered in a crate stamped ACME,
to unpack Nietzsche's notion of Eternal Return – *beep, beep!* –
to fail, to fall, to heal into elasticity, to fight
again and again, to cantilever the boulder of No-Can-Do,
to launch the kit-built, heat-seeking missile of Love, its Circular Error
        Probability,
the heat it seeks in me, my scorched eye-sockets burning
with acrid gas, my aim
unerring as always to get that hen
– *beep-beep!* – Take 10. Pass me that pellet of peyote.

IV *Ode to Karen Black*

Apparently, five-finger exercises on a piano roped to the back
of a moving pick-up truck is one sure sign of a wandering Muse,
which might, at any moment, dump you in Puget Sound or Salt-Lake
City, ambition thinned to a salt lick
on the wind, a wind that sifts the eelgrass,
gets sifted in turn by windsocks, oil derricks into an anodyne blur.
He who wheeled his stroke-silenced father into a field
for a one-sided conversation
knows he has to encrypt

the gaps in this shooting-script
with his own DNA. Our woman tunes out to a Country station,
blousy gingham apron bulging with gold,
half-Julie Christie, half-Ben Turpin as she is, determined to demur.
O oddball Goddess in plunge-line, see-thru nightdress,
who feels the kick inside that anchors everything, or loosens it, or leaves it
            to Lady Luck.
A night-lit filling station. A logging-truck. They say over yonder, 'desire'
            is spurred by 'lack'
but everything, like your gaze, goes both ways
Karen Black.

Eleven Gallons in a Ten-gallon Hat

...if memory is recovery,
forgetfulness theft,
recall then Wallace Beery
most often the third cowboy
on the left;
if not, maybe Jack Elam
squinting at the quizzical sun,
dying time after time
in Tombstone or Tucson
Arizona, zoning out. The cacti may flower
in slo-mo, whole prairies shift,
but Noah or Wallace Beery
is always that third cowboy
on the left. *Apparently.*

Domesticity

Apparently, the picture Jesse James is trying to adjust,
– its slightly skew-whiff frame, its inch-thick of dust –
is an original Magritte, that one of a man in a bowler hat
looking at the back of another man in a bowler hat,

or the very same one, whatever.
Whatever, the hunched back of the antimacassar
bears witness as he rights the picture-plane, his eye like a spirit-level.
He smells a coyote out on the town boundary. He smells its growl.

Yet the offices of a good wife,
the smotherings of children, the warm arms of the good life
have so dulled those stirrings of the nape-fur particular to his ilk, he never
        notices confrère Robert Ford, spry in bowler hat,
set down rawlplug and mirror-plate,
reacquaint himself with his inner coward,
gently let down his friend, then go out to tell the neighbourhood.

Abandoned Winnebago Camper

Apparently, if not him, who'd have thought
of this abandoned Winnebago-camper
reeling on its side in a ditch
stitched with clover? Or the tall, *Stetson*'d woman leaning on the hood,
      the driver,
elbowing out her double, that swimmer
rising up through flash-floods of mercury,
– that's mercury as Hg NO6, not the planet nor Mercury Rev's *Girl on*
      a Highway –
or that hare's paw hanging from dash, that water-moccasin,
or her daughter

wearing purple knee-socks or knee-deep in the clover
that edges the four-lane
freeway
as she dashes out to catch a zigzagging bee?
Me, for one. For a vast emptiness can nest inside the vastest happiness –
      or vice-versa –
as a last ditch after-thought or precursor
to being sat in this ersatz, All-Nite diner, eyes stretched
by the wall-mounted chrome bumper of some long abandoned Winnebago-
      camper
wringing the tail-end of a seven-year itch. Ditch it.

The Quarrel

Apparently, sorrel and sagebrush, mountain-laurel
from a canyon like a gap inside the mind.

Pacific ocean wind –
a strand as long as the aftermath of a quarrel.

Two frozen Daiquiris left out upon the taffrail
as indolent salt-lines map the sand.

Doc Holliday coughs blood into his hand-
kerchief, sidles into the OK Corral.

Ok. He takes his 4/10 and cleans out both barrels.
The night-girls from the crib draw down the blinds

but open up a canyon in his mind
full of mountain-laurel, sagebrush and wild sorrel.

Acquiescence

Apparently, we crossed that tawdry snowline
to come upon a lynx in an ice-hung hawthorn, then another, or the same
         one again
by a lightning-struck pine.
The cold was a presence.
When the dog squatted to pee
its pee became a little sheeted lake. By an icicle-fringed gulley
Fontainebleau let slip about the bodies,
and a little further up we found a cairn, then an improvised sepulchre.
We prised the biggest slab but nothing grinned back at us – just foetid air.

Without jewellery, descending through dank copses, I thought of Clytemnestra,
the pearl-string glimmering on her chest;
how amongst the All-Nite girls from the *Mobil* garage, none could best her

for heft or malevolence. Our furs became coral. The cold grew inside us like
         a worm.
The dog died trying to shit a snowball. The gulley took its whine.
A warm voice called out to us. It felt like acquiescence.

Illinois Ode

Apparently, Illinois
there you lay before us like a flood-plain,
cinquefoil and scrub upon your verges – *asperges me* –
vulnerable as we were to unseen forces,
drill-bit twisters, Biblical rains;
that and your hydroelectric dams, fantails, clicking insects.
Illinois, I loved you and
you left me while I slept.

O Illinois,
there you lay before us like a 10 cent demimondaine
cometh the hour, cometh the man, etc. – O the urges! –
rainfall being a factor in, say, 40% of divorces,
that and your wrecked wheelbarrows, aforementioned twisters, alluvial plains,
thunder calling Collect.
Illinois, I loved you and
you left me while I slept.

Apparently, Illinois
there you lay before us like a derailed train,
our speech-patterns proto-Algonquian, Wabash surges
in spate. Your running-boards, horse-drawn hearses;
these and Decatur, Bloomington Normal, Port Vincennes
dotting the map to castigate Little Egypt.
Illinois, I loved you and
you left me while I slept.

O Illinois,
your wind-farms in the Grain Belt lay the weather-vanes,
hail Peoria – social and cultural belle weather, good burghers
horde their State Flower Violets and whomsoever coerces
them coerces the white-tailed deer, their scrape-lines
scenting the hickory, scentings that the hickories accept.
Illinois, I loved you and
you left me while I slept.

Apparently, Illinois
there you lay before us like the floor plan
for some forty-storey car park, your flat-packs, green-lipped mussels,
        AOR dirges;
all your ladies husbanding their resources;
that and your horsetail waterfalls plunging into drains
leaving no one's dignity intact.
Illinois, I loved you and
you left me while I slept.

The Ballad of Bay Mare

Apparently, Buckminster Fuller deigned
a geodesic dome for Santa Fe
seaward of where his shrimp-boat, bobbing in the bay,
was tethered by its single, fraying rope.
So what if I came ashore to scout that freckled bluff,
its plunge-line of loose-footed scree
falling to a bed of chaff and buddleia
where the lone, lean, fine bare mare was rollicking?

I careered around that corner, purblind and sun-screened
smack-dab into the King of Spain's daughter, her eyes like anti-freeze.
For her stolid courtiers to tell me fate is a lousy lay.

Hey, eastward the sea and a light-struck skiff
are lapping against each other, insistently,
but the distance remains the distance from *here to there*, bay mare.

To a Dead Fly on the Mirror-sill

(from the Czech of Ferda Mravenec)

Apparently, you're making as if to take flight
green iridescence, blue iridescence
trembling in your wings, up-ended as you are by the tube of Colgate,
but it's merely the sly, sideways breeze
from the cracked bathroom window. As a termite mound
shows exactly as much on the surface
as is burrowed below the ground,
so does my face

reveal as much of my own true will
as is hidden behind it. The serrated firs on the incline
their blue iridescence, green iridescence – sway under clouds and swall-

ows as the razor leaves my chin
for my Adam's apple. O comrade, inert fly on the mirror-sill, by the pills
and many medicines.

Cloudburst

Apparently "gallery-attendant" is a dead-end job,
your peripheral vision gilded by cloud-bank angst,
the odd philanthropist
come in out the rain.

Your back's pre-written
by the cane chair's mesh and, there's the rub,
it cannot sieve the tension
from your shoulder-blades. You're neither host nor guest.

Jacob
is there also, straining against
his beautiful antagonist – *three falls, two submissions* –
who, like a patient instructor, lets him strain.

This Voice

Apparently, this voice ushers up from somewhere inside this body,
some deep intestinal rumble below which ever sonar
cannot go. Its decibels vibrate
in the legs of tables, that Ottoman-scroll chaise-longue, this chair
in which Mercy splays, apparently pose-less, all listless disarray,
a nipple by an elbow, an ankle by an ear, that choker
holding back her throat as though speech
were an impertinence.
This voice has the breathless duty

to consider each fractal of her beauty,
its grain and gravel. Yet it goes deeper, way beyond rebuff or acquiescence
into the floorboards, the wood grain, the skirting where that roach
skrik-skriks micro-legs at a level so low even a basso-profundo might choke,
hold and delay
but not go lower, lower being beneath the coffin-lids where no one is aware
of this voice intoning prayers like a drowsy prelate.
Though notice how one of the dead here has a boner,
even entirely asleep he wants her so badly.

Barefoot Boy

Apparently, he's never been, exactly, the barefoot boy, some fly
sand-stepper in silted espadrilles
afloat – cut off *contra-naturam* by his underpowered *Sony-Walkman*
playing, as it is today, Stockhausen's *Helicopter Quartet*,
the sound of which is the whole ocean distilled into a pipette
or a hornet over the water.
The word stopping his mouth is oftimes 'partisan'
or 'gift' or 'elsewhere', not barefootedness as timidity
but plangent caution, the beach, being as it is, sharp with obsidian.

Not that the sea's desultory sparks are any kind of obsession,
far from it, in fact his romantic idyll's a pig-sty,
in fact, his blundering shocks a part-feathered ptarmigan
out of the couch-grass, an exploding avatar
full of 4/10 buckshot.
If he'd tried for a decade he'd never have winged it with a conscious potshot,
his mind lacy as the sea's hem,
it saying 'What now?' 'What now, indeed', ponders Pindar and his irreducible
        double,
'What now for the barefoot boy?'

The Intimacy of Ishmael and Queequeg

Apparently, the co-joining of sea-salt and cannibal,
of a lapsed believer and a gurning God
so as to placate the cold, now strikes us as beautiful.
In the swaying hammocks of the *Pequod*,
so much might be made of Ishmael and Queequeg,
this intimacy, ploughing through vast meadows of brit,
league upon league
like boundless fields of wheat,
such details as do not make the Captain's log,
of those who favour cabin fever
over the law of the bail and the tether-peg
the winch and the cantilever
who bestride the deck,
both stowaway and counterfoil
tread the reconstructed splinters of this wreck,
then don the whale's
foreskin as if it were a cagoule,
who foreswear the warmth of a snore, of an armpit
where brawny tendril
segues into brawny tendril to indicate
a merging, ecumenical,
beyond gender, lust, or intrigue
though guy-rope fray guy-rope in the fo'c'sle,
The Leviathan leaping in clover, Ahab in rehab, dogged
by the ghost of each other – say, Palestine and Israel –
as the tattooed route-map writ on a cannibal's leg
segues into the veins of a Christian arm, holds out against the whale,
the intimacy of Ishmael and Queequeg.

The Argument

Apparently, contrary to popular belief,
it's land that makes advances on the ocean,
time and time again, the brink of a bluff
speckled with wet bayberry, juniper, split larch
sallies forth as the tide retreats, possessive only of stone,
and yet again, stone. As its back begins to arch,
troubled at the root, the Spit advance-
s, high with spate, with föhn,
and waits, as land waits, buoyed up by subsidence
building beneath. It's the ocean will always rescind
flounces, laces, forget-me-knots and favours, its backbone
of gilded spray at the least caprice of wind.
One night-star as referee,
and even then, alone,
averse to risk, the thinnest air seeming airy
in such company. The stand-off absolute. Only then does the ocean return
with its girdles of kelp, its sloughed-off shoulders of foam
to lap and lick the minerals, make moan
until the bluff is less a bluff
and more a quarry, the quarry less a quarry than a slum,
the slam of advancing land and inward ocean, their continuous rift
like Olson's *theory of continental drift*
wherein the Shenandoah once ran through County Durham,
the Belgian Congo through Angel, Islington,
the Ohio through a Carshalton Beeches car park, the sinuous Elbe along
        the M21,
the Lusatian Neisse through the palisades of Peckham,
the Niff through nowhere, the Yangtze through Hither Green,
the Susquehanna through the watercourses of Camden;
and the source of the Nile is Plato Road, Brixton,
contrary to popular belief.

The Bluff

Apparently, the lights are in scatter-fall above the bluff,
its incline serrated by firs
into dark-green saw teeth,
thence a slither of wortleberry and scree to where
the bay bulges into the ocean like a breathalysing balloon,
dotted by a single dhow or skiff
– from here it's not quite clear – which is where our guts go airborne.
Barely tethered to the wild, green globe itself

the skiff is held by only a fraying lily-rope
to a spar of shingle, as if either might drift off, where, under a wind-
        tugged tarp
the Great Master is trying to map

the impalpable auroras. He must depend, fences not being enough,
on these few illegible scribbles holding off
the scatter fall of evening. And therein lies the bluff.

Pancreas

Apparently, biology is mostly internal,
what hangs inside the body – intestinal, interminable,
slithery yet palpable, what makes us capable
of being – is, to us, outside ourselves as it were, invisible,
fibre-optics not withstanding. See here the lungs, one slightly bronchial,
        the stain visible:
an image of the Rue de Quatrefrages or an ideogram of Pocatello, Idaho.
        I've yet to go. Yet these risible
lungs do daily blow, expand, exhale
without, of course, inhaling. Get me a Pataphysician such as Monsieur
        Queneau to tell
it as it isn't, or a Tel Quel to unpick the body politic. If all else fails

the body of work, the work of the body prevails, even dissembled as soil.
        Some hole inside us the insides fill
the duodenum that knows where it's coming from, the small intestine
        pristine as a well,
the lumbar region, insulin and glucagons, the veins, the ventricles all

hanging tough. It's invidious but, if asked to pick a body-part I will,
invariably, whilst not entirely overlooking your ass, plump for the pancreas.
        That's all.